ANATOMY CLASS

THE Human Skeleton

by Jody Sullivan Rake

Consultant:
Marjorie J. Hogan, MD
Associate Professor
University of Minnesota, Minneapolis

Capstone press®

Mankato, Minnesota

Fact Finders is published by Capstone Press,
151 Good Counsel Drive, P.O. Box 669, Mankato, Minnesota 56002.
www.capstonepress.com

Library of Congress Cataloging-in-Publication Data
Rake, Jody Sullivan
    Human skeleton / by Jody Sullivan Rake.
    p. cm. — (Fact finders. Anatomy class)
    Includes bibliographical references and index.
    Summary: "Describes the human skeleton, including connective tissues, bone growth and
repair" — Provided by publisher.
    ISBN 978-1-4296-3340-6 (library binding)
    ISBN 978-1-4296-3888-3 (softcover)
    1. Human skeleton — Juvenile literature. I. Title. II. Series.
QM101.R35 2010
611'.71 — dc22   2009002771

Editorial Credits
Lori Shores, editor; Ted Williams, designer; Svetlana Zhurkin, media researcher

Photo Credits
Alamy/Phototake, 20 (inset)
Getty Images/3D4Medical, 17, 25, 29; Nucleus Medical Art, 9; Visuals Unlimited/Dr. Don Fawcett, 19
Peter Arnold/Lobo Press International, 7
Photo Researchers/Living Art Enterprises, 23
Phototake/Helene Fournie, 20
Shutterstock/Claudio Bertoloni, 17 (inset); Franc Podgoršek, 11; Galina Barskaya, 26;
    Larry St. Pierre, 25 (inset); Oguz Aral, 13 (inset); Peter Weber, 5; Sebastian Kaulitzki, cover,
    11 (inset), 13, 14

Essential content terms are **bold** and are defined at the bottom of the page where they first appear.

Table of Contents

A Solid Framework

Imagine a skyscraper made without a framework of steel. Would the building hold up against a bad storm? Sturdy frameworks give buildings shape and provide support. The 206 bones of your skeleton provide the framework for your body. Without a skeleton, you would be a shapeless blob. Your height, shape, and the length of your **limbs** all depend on your skeleton.

Together with your muscles, your skeleton helps you move. But that's not all it does. The skeleton is a living part of your body. Deep inside, your bones make blood cells that keep you healthy. By itself, a skeleton might look a little scary, but it's not. The human skeleton is an amazing combination of strength and balance.

limb — an arm or leg

BODY FACT

The skeleton also protects your internal organs. Your rib bones form a "cage" around your lungs and heart.

CHAPTER 1

Under the Skin

If you peeled off your skin, you wouldn't see your bones underneath. Your skeleton is hidden under muscles and connective tissues. These tissues attach bones to muscles and other bones.

Tendons and ligaments are tough, cordlike connective tissues. Ligaments hold your bones together so they don't pop out of place. Tendons attach muscles to bones. Flexing a muscle pulls on the tendon, like a bungee cord. Then the tendon pulls on the bone to move it. When you flex your upper arm muscle, strong tendons pull your forearm up.

Cartilage adds padding between bones to protect them from rubbing together. This strong, rubbery tissue also gives shape where there are no bones. Your outer ears and the lower half of your nose are made of cartilage. Rub your nose and gently wiggle it. You can feel where your nose bone ends and your cartilage begins.

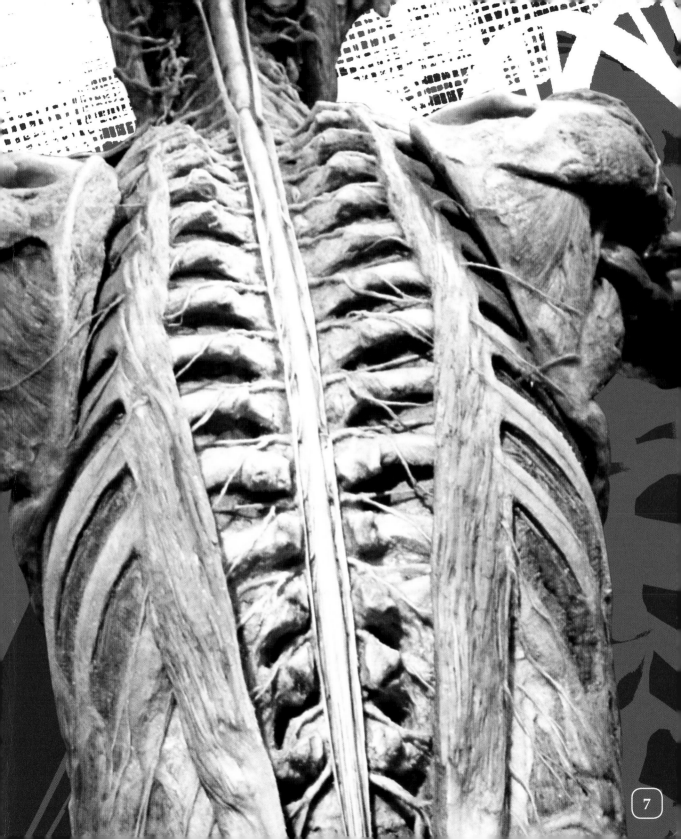

Where Bones Get Together

If you could look under all those connective tissues, you would see how your bones fit together. The place where two or more bones meet is called a joint. But joints are much more than two bones coming together. Without joints, you wouldn't be able to jump, run, or move at all. You can move because of your joints and the muscles that power them.

Protective capsules surround moving joints. These capsules are filled with a thick, slippery fluid to keep joints moving smoothly. For even more protection, the ends of the bones are padded with cartilage.

BODY FACT

Some joints don't move at all. Most of your skull bones can't move. The joints in your backbone only move a little bit.

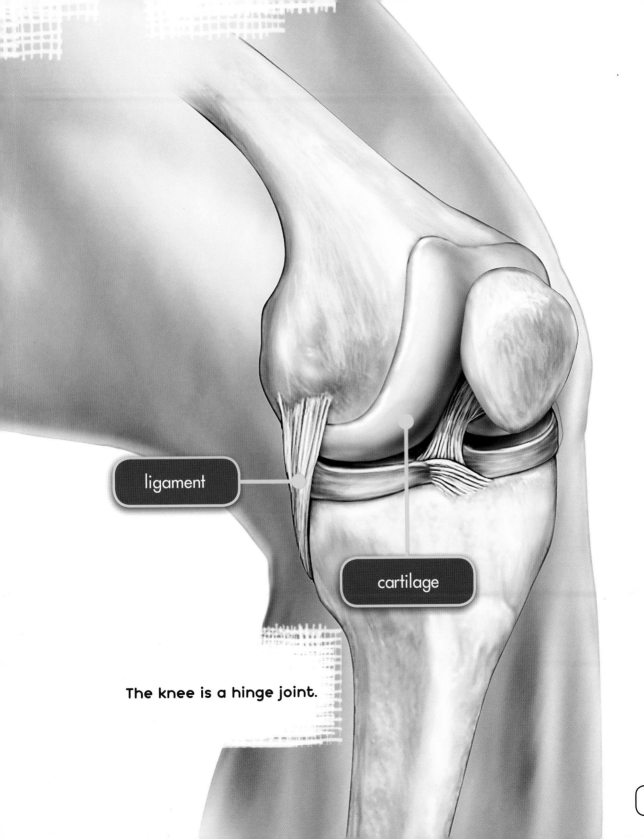

ligament

cartilage

The knee is a hinge joint.

Jump for Joy over Joints

The many joints of your skeleton allow you to move in different ways. Thanks to your joints, you can throw a football or use a hula hoop. Each type of joint is named for what it looks like or how it works.

Ball-and-socket joints allow bones to move in all directions, like a video game joystick. The rounded head of one bone fits into a hollow space, or socket, of another. In your hip, the head of the **femur** fits into a socket in the **pelvis**.

Hinge joints move bones forward and backward. These joints join two bones together like a door hinge. Your knee and elbow joints are hinge joints.

In a pivot joint, one bone turns around part of another bone. The head and neck form a pivot joint. This joint allows you to turn your head from side to side.

> **femur** — the bone that extends from the pelvis to the knee
> **pelvis** — the large bony structure near the base of the spine where the legs attach

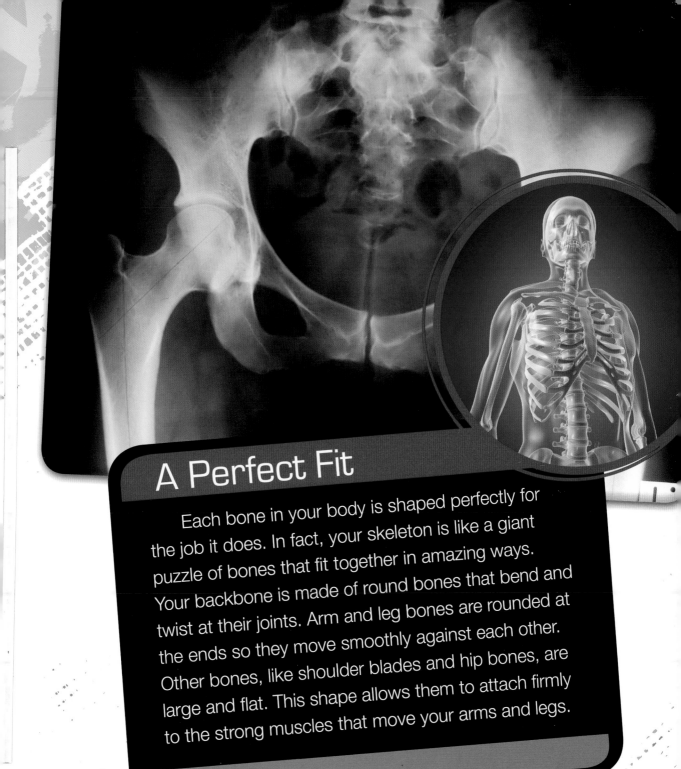

A Perfect Fit

Each bone in your body is shaped perfectly for the job it does. In fact, your skeleton is like a giant puzzle of bones that fit together in amazing ways. Your backbone is made of round bones that bend and twist at their joints. Arm and leg bones are rounded at the ends so they move smoothly against each other. Other bones, like shoulder blades and hip bones, are large and flat. This shape allows them to attach firmly to the strong muscles that move your arms and legs.

CHAPTER 2

Boning Up on Bones

Once you get past muscles and connective tissues, you're left with the bare bones. Tap on the top of your head. Pretty solid, right? Skull bones are strong to protect your brain. You can't move these bones. Of the 29 bones that make up your skull, only the lower jawbone moves.

Leading down from your skull, your backbone is strong and tall like a tree trunk. These 26 bumpy bones fit together to support your body. They also protect your **spinal cord**.

Take a deep breath. Did your ribs move? Your 24 ribs are connected by cartilage that keeps them in place to protect your lungs. But the cartilage also stretches so your ribs can move. The ribs move just enough to allow your lungs to fill with air.

> **spinal cord** — the bundle of nerves and tissues that connects all parts of the body to the brain

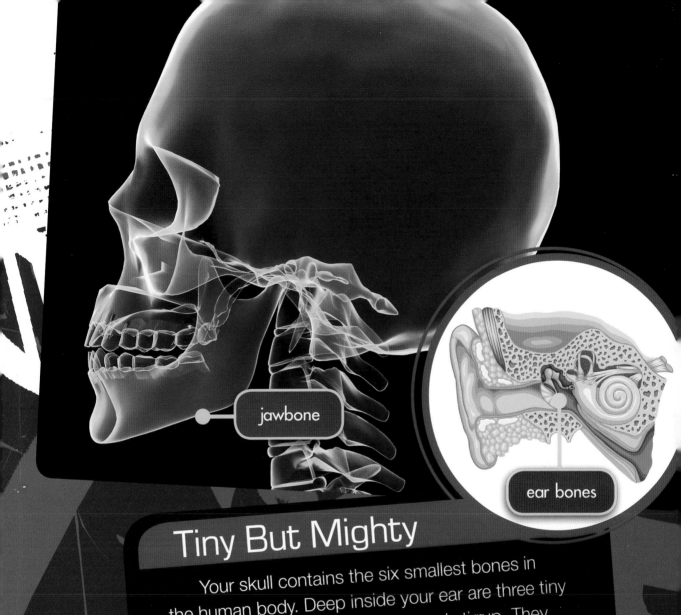

jawbone

ear bones

Tiny But Mighty

Your skull contains the six smallest bones in the human body. Deep inside your ear are three tiny bones called the hammer, anvil, and stirrup. They are named for their shapes. These bones may be tiny, but they do a big job. They help carry sound waves to the brain.

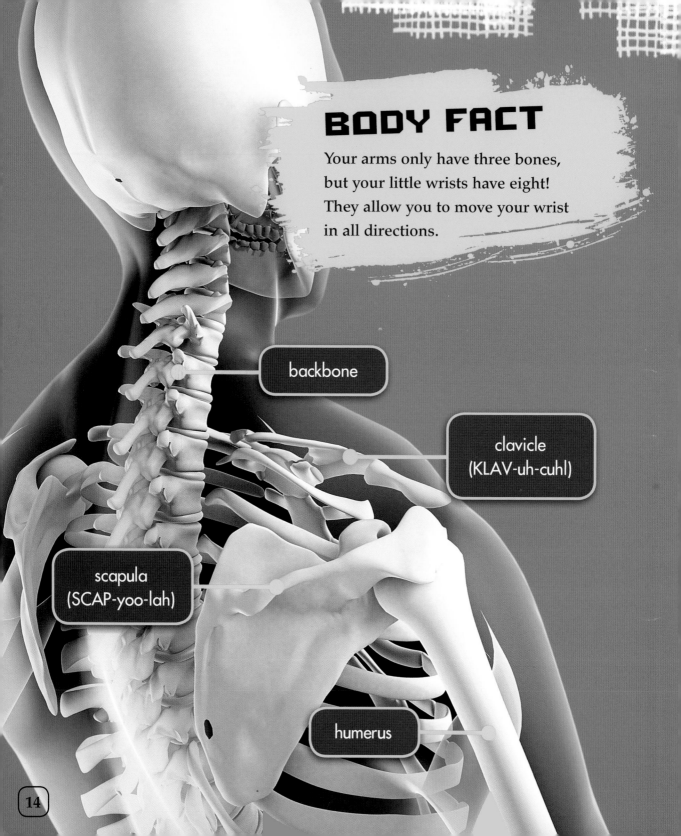

BODY FACT

Your arms only have three bones, but your little wrists have eight! They allow you to move your wrist in all directions.

backbone

clavicle
(KLAV-uh-cuhl)

scapula
(SCAP-yoo-lah)

humerus

Arms Wide Open

Your arms connect to your skeleton at your shoulders. Scapulas, or shoulder blades, have round grooves where the upper arm bone fits. Clavicles, or collarbones, are shaped like a long S to hold your shoulder joints away from your body. This allows you to move your arms in more ways.

What's humorous about the humerus? The humerus is the long bone that runs from your shoulder to your elbow. Have you ever bumped that spot on your elbow that makes your arm feel dead? People call that hitting your "funny bone." But really it's a nerve in your elbow that causes the loss of feeling.

The two bones of your lower arm, the radius and ulna, do a cool trick. When you hold your palm up, the bones run side by side. When you turn your palm down, they form an "X" as one bone flips over the other. These bones make turning a doorknob possible.

A Strong Support System

Every day, your pelvis carries a lot of weight. Sitting, standing, even lying down, your pelvis helps support you. Its wide, curved shape cradles your **torso**. This shape also allows you to walk on two legs.

The farther down you go, the more weight that part of the skeleton supports. Running and jumping put a lot of stress on the leg bones. The thick bones of the legs are super strong. Your femurs are the longest and heaviest bones in your body. Buried deep in muscles, the femur is one of the few bones you can't feel through your skin.

But your legs don't do all the work. With each step, your feet support all of your weight. The arching shape of the foot is the best shape for supporting weight. That's why architects use the arch design to add strength to their structures.

> **torso** — the part of the body between the neck and waist

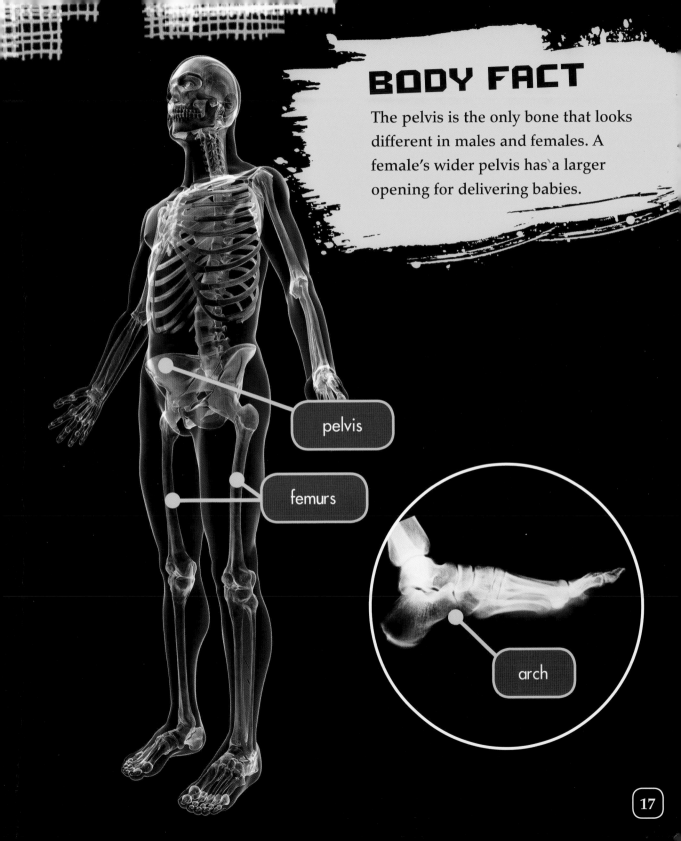

The pelvis is the only bone that looks different in males and females. A female's wider pelvis has a larger opening for delivering babies.

pelvis

femurs

arch

CHAPTER 3

A Closer Look at Bone

From the top of your skull to the tips of your toes, your skeleton is an engineering wonder. But inside those hard bones is a whole world of activity.

If you could peel back the smooth surface of a bone, you would find a thick layer of compact bone. The compact bone is made up of **calcium** and strong, bendy **collagen**. Calcium makes bones hard. Collagen makes bones hard to break.

At the ends of long bones you'll find spongy bone. Like a sponge, this type of bone is full of air spaces. But unlike a sponge, spongy bone is hard. The weblike pattern of bony "beams" adds strength to the bone and keeps it from being too heavy.

calcium — a soft mineral needed for strong teeth and bones
collagen — a protein found in connective tissues, skin, and bones

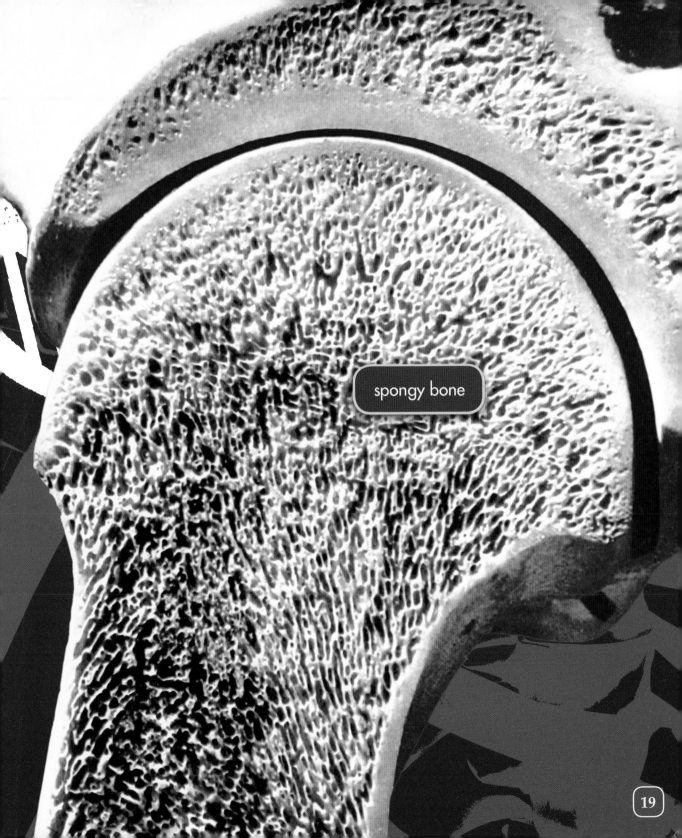

spongy bone

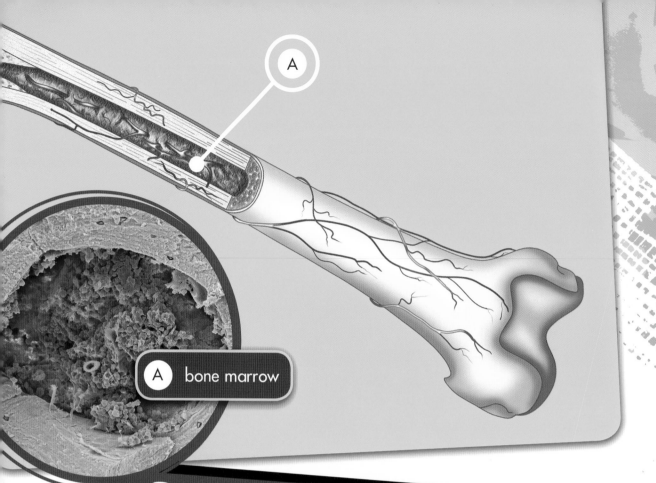

Crack!

If you break a bone, your doctor may put it in a cast. But the cast just keeps everything in place. The bone itself does the work of healing. When a bone breaks, bone cells gather around the break and make callus, a form of bone material. Over time, the bone cells make strong bone material from the callus. In just a few weeks, the bone is as good as new again.

Living Bones

Although we often think of bones as nonliving objects, they are actually living, growing tissue. Inside the compact bone, tiny tubes run the length of the bone. The tubes contain blood vessels that supply blood and oxygen to the bone cells.

Deep inside, the centers of your large bones are fairly hollow. This hollow space is called the marrow cavity. Compared to the smooth, white outer bone, the marrow cavity looks fuzzy and red. But this isn't just empty space. Inside the marrow cavity, jellylike bone marrow does important work. Bone marrow makes blood cells that carry oxygen through the body and fight infection. It also makes cells called platelets that help blood to clot.

BODY FACT

Every second, bone marrow produces about 2 million red blood cells.

Bone Growth

You can thank your bones each time your favorite pants get too short on you. The ends of your long bones, like arms and legs, contain small amounts of cartilage. The cartilage slowly turns to bone as you get older. As long as there is cartilage, the bone continues to grow. By the time you are an adult, all the cartilage is replaced by bone. Your bones then stop growing.

Bones grow thicker too. Special cells build bone layers from the outside in. But the marrow cavity needs to grow too. Other cells break down bone from the inside. As the bones grow on the outside, the inside breaks down to keep the bone at just the right thickness.

BODY FACT

Bone layers look like the rings of a tree. But because old bone is broken down, people don't have one ring for each year of life like trees.

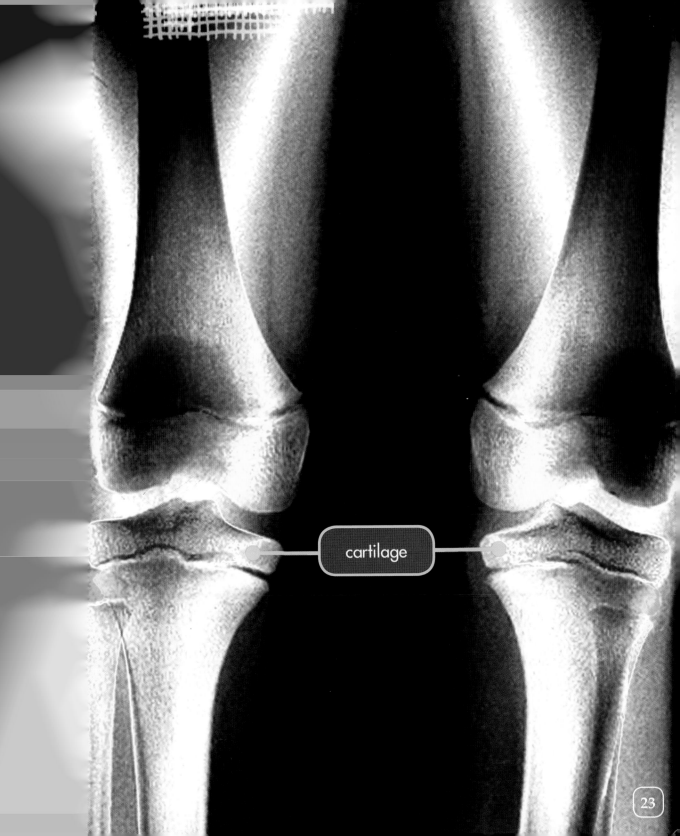

cartilage

CHAPTER 4

A Healthy Skeleton

Your bones take care of you if you take care of them. A healthy diet is important for bone health. Calcium and vitamin D help keep your bones healthy and strong. Milk and other dairy products are a good source of these important nutrients. Sunlight is also a good source of vitamin D.

Your bones can take a lot of stress, but they do have their breaking point. How easily a bone can break, or fracture, depends on diet, physical condition, health, and age. The bones of children don't break as easily as those of older people. Children's bones also heal faster when they do break.

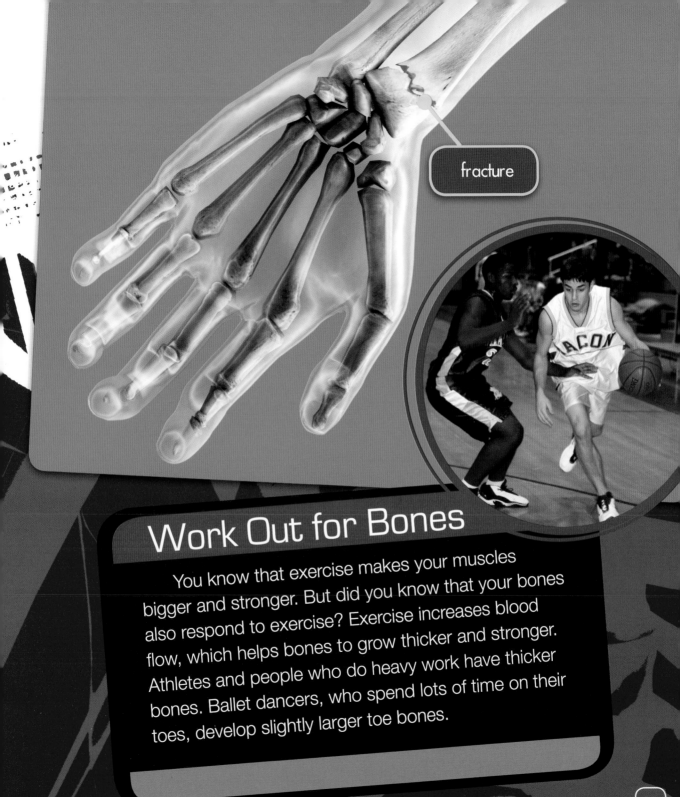

fracture

Work Out for Bones

You know that exercise makes your muscles bigger and stronger. But did you know that your bones also respond to exercise? Exercise increases blood flow, which helps bones to grow thicker and stronger. Athletes and people who do heavy work have thicker bones. Ballet dancers, who spend lots of time on their toes, develop slightly larger toe bones.

Super Skeleton

Your incredible skeleton is always working. It keeps you strong and on the move. Whether you are standing, sitting, or running, your skeleton gives you support and protection. Even if you are lying perfectly still, your tiny ear bones are working, sending sound to your brain.

Your bones are stronger than steel but still light enough to let you move around. Many features of the skeleton have been copied to build better buildings and other structures. But no structure could ever match the wonders of the human skeleton.

BODY FACT

Bone is strong but light. A steel beam the same size as a bone would weigh four times as much!

Skeleton Diagram

A — **Skull** — Your face alone has 14 bones.

B — **Jawbone** — The jawbone holds your lower teeth in place.

C — **Backbone** — The 26 bones of the backbone are called vertebrae.

D — **Ribs** — Most people have 12 pairs of rib bones, but a few people have an extra pair.

E — **Pelvis** — The pelvis is made of six bones joined together.

F — **Femur** — The femur, or thighbone, makes up about one fourth of your total height.

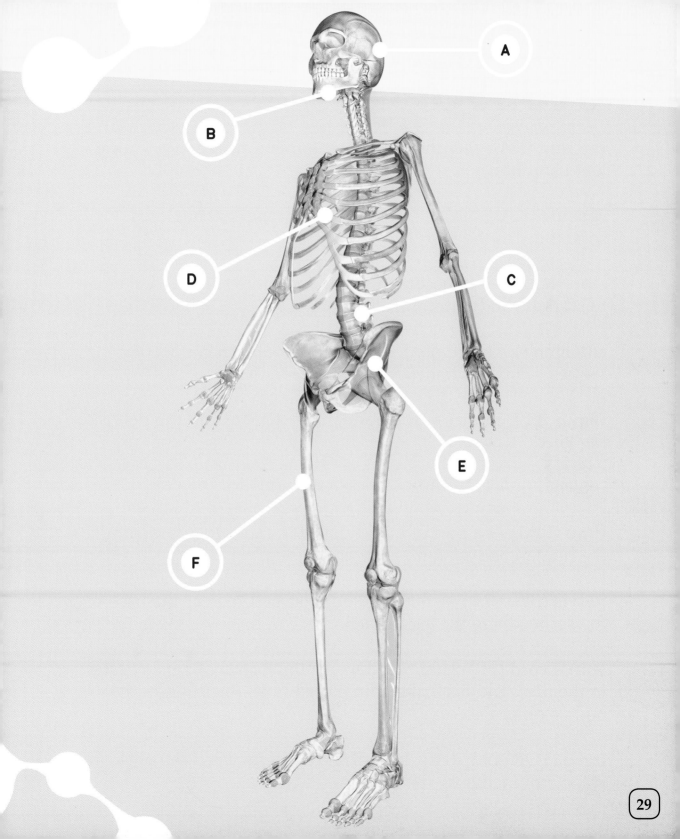

Glossary

calcium (KAL-see-uhm) — a soft mineral needed for strong teeth and bones

capsule (KAP-suhl) — a tough membrane that encloses something in the body

clot (KLOT) — to become thicker and more solid; blood clots to stop the body from bleeding.

collagen (CALL-uh-jen) — a protein found in connective tissues, skin, and bones

femur (FEE-muhr) — the bone that extends from the pelvis to the knee

internal (in-TUR-nuhl) — inside the body

limb (LIM) — a part of a body used in moving or grasping; in the human body, a limb is an arm or leg.

pelvis (PEL-viss) — the large bony structure near the base of the spine where the legs attach

spinal cord (SPY-nuhl KORD) — a thick cord of nerve tissue in the neck and back; the spinal cord links the brain to the body's other nerves.

torso (TOR-soh) — the part of the body between the neck and waist, not including the arms

Read More

Barraclough, Sue. *The Skeletal and Muscular Systems: How Can I Stand On My Head?* Body Systems. Chicago: Heinemann, 2008.

Jakab, Cheryl. *The Skeletal System.* Our Body. North Mankato, Minn.: Smart Apple Media, 2006.

Stewart, Gregory J. *The Skeletal and Muscular Systems.* The Human Body: How It Works. New York: Chelsea House, 2009.

Internet Sites

FactHound offers a safe, fun way to find Internet sites related to this book. All of the sites on FactHound have been researched by our staff.

Here's all you do:

Visit *www.facthound.com*

FactHound will fetch the best sites for you!

Index